I Like Beetles

by GLADYS CONKLIN

pictures by JEAN ZALLINGER

Holiday House . New York

For John Briggs,
whose empathy
is ever present

A companion volume to
I LIKE BUTTERFLIES
I LIKE CATERPILLARS
WE LIKE BUGS

*Specimens of the beetles illustrated were loaned
to the artist by the Peabody Museum of Yale University
and by the University of California at Berkeley.*

Text copyright © 1975 by Gladys Conklin
Illustrations copyright © 1975 by Jean Zallinger
All rights reserved
Printed in the United States of America

Library of Congress Cataloging in Publication Data
Conklin, Gladys Plemon.
I like beetles.
SUMMARY: Briefly describes the distinguishing characteristics of twenty-nine types of beetles.
1. Beetles—Juvenile literature. [1. Beetles]
I. Zallinger, Jean Day, ill. II. Title.
QL576.2.C65   595.7´6   75-4728
ISBN 0-8234-0262-2

I like beetles.
  I find them everywhere.
  Big ones that move slowly
  like heavy trucks,
  small ones that speed along
  like little sports cars,
  and tiny ones that take off
  and fly like little airplanes.
  I like all beetles.

A tiger beetle is beautiful
in its spotted blue and green coat.
It can run so fast that it
can catch almost anything.
I wanted it to stay but it
kept running and ran away.
I think maybe
it can run faster than I can.

TIGER BEETLE

Click beetles are like clowns.
I turn one over on its back
and watch. It slowly bends in
the middle. I jump as it goes *click!*
and pops into the air.
It turns over and lands on its
feet. I wish I could do that.

CLICK BEETLE

I was walking across a field when I saw a bright red spot on a flower.
It was a fire-colored beetle.
I stared and stared at its wonderful feelers.
I never saw anything like them on other beetles.

FIRE-COLORED BEETLE

A black bombardier beetle was in
my path. I moved closer
and it stood on its head.
Pop! and out shot a puff of
vapor from the end of its body.
It smells like a skunk.
Its enemies run and so do I.

BOMBARDIER BEETLE

I go to the creek and
wade where the water
is ankle-deep.
The whirligigs are dancing
around and around.
When a cloud covers the sun
they disappear.

WHIRLIGIG BEETLE

There are diving beetles
in our pond.
I saw a grasshopper fall
into the water.
A big water beetle
caught it and
pulled it under.

PREDACEOUS DIVING BEETLE

I saw a small golden spot
on a green leaf.
It was a tiny goldbug.
It flew away so fast that
I didn't see its wings open.

The ladybug in my hand plays dead. I watch one tiny little leg after another slowly uncurl. The ladybug rocks gently from side to side until it turns over. Its lacy wings unfold and it flies away.

LADYBUG

I found a beautiful dead
alder beetle on the ground.
I picked it up carefully
and carried it home.
I'll keep it in a little box
and look at it every day.

ALDER BEETLE

There's a dead mouse in the garden. I'm watching the burying beetles put it under the ground. They dig under its body. It sinks lower and lower until it's covered up.

BURYING BEETLE OR SEXTON BEETLE

TUMBLEBUG

I watched a tumblebug pushing a ball of food up a hill. The ball slipped and went rolling down, dragging the beetle with it. The tumblebug tried again and again before it reached the top of that hill.

FIREFLY

On warm summer evenings the meadow is full of magic lights. The fireflies are talking. I like to catch a firefly and hold it in my hand for a few minutes. It's fun to watch the light go on and off between my fingers.

JUNE BUG

On summer evenings when the lights are on, I hear a *wump!* against the screen door. The June bugs are flying. The bright light invites them to come inside. They try and try but the screen door is always in the way.

There's a street light in front of our house. On summer evenings I like to explore under the light. Once a giant water beetle landed right at my feet. I put it in a jar so I could look at it. The next morning I took it to the pond and turned it loose.

WATER SCAVENGER BEETLE

I like to touch
the green flower beetle.
Its back looks like soft velvet
but it feels like a hard shell.
It's beautiful but it's a
pest on our fig trees.
My father calls it a fig-eater.

GROUND BEETLE

I saw a long line of tracks
going up a sandy hill.
It looked as if a tiny tractor
had climbed the hill.
I went up the hill and found
a shiny black ground beetle.

I like the mighty caterpillar-hunter. It climbs trees to hunt for caterpillars. When it finds a nest of tent caterpillars, it eats and eats hundreds of them in one day.

CATERPILLAR HUNTER
OR
FIERY SEARCHER

I like to watch the grand
stag beetle. It sucks sap from the
leaking bark of an oak tree.
Its huge jaws
are like heavy antlers.
When it walks
it looks as if it's
going to topple over.

STAG BEETLE

PRIONUS BEETLE

The big prionus beetle won't play with me. When I touch it gently with my finger, it doesn't like it. The prionus rubs his hind legs against his hard wings and makes a loud scratching noise that means "Leave me alone."

Farmers don't like the potato beetles. They eat the leaves of the potato plants. When there are too many beetles, they eat all the leaves and the plants die.

COLORADO POTATO BEETLE

I've looked lots of times but I've never found a Japanese beetle.
I guess we're lucky.
If I ever find one, I'll take it to my mother or father. It's a beetle that eats up people's gardens.
I hope I never find one.

JAPANESE BEETLE

0.4"

The ten-lined June beetle has silver lines on its back. When it's disturbed, its graceful feelers open like tiny fans. I tickle it with a straw and it squeaks in a shrill voice.

JUNE BEETLE

COTTONWOOD BORER

The cottonwood borer is
a sturdy beetle,
all shiny black and white.
When it hides under a leaf,
its long waving feelers
show me where to find it.

I found a red milkweed beetle on a milkweed plant. The monarch butterfly feeds on the milkweed plant too. It woul be exciting to find both of them on the same plant. I'll keep looking, and someday I'll find them together.

MILKWEED BEETLE

The net-winged beetle lives on flowers. It's easy to find it because it has bright orange and black colors. I touched its wings. They aren't hard like most beetles' wings—they're soft.

NET-WINGED BEETLE

The spotted tree borer is one of my favorite beetles. It's small, and comfortable to hold in my hand. Its long feelers wave back and forth as if it's being friendly.

SPOTTED TREE BORER

The pine sawyer beetle lives on trees. Its feelers are more than twice as long as its body. I wonder if they get in the way when it crawls through the pine needles.

PINE SAWYER BEETLE

I saw a wonderful beetle on my vacation. He had a head like a small dinosaur and he's called a rhinoceros beetle. I stretched out my hand and touched his strange horns. I liked the feel of them.

RHINOCEROS BEETLE

The Goliath beetle is almost as big as my hand. It lives in the trees in Africa. When it opens its huge wings, it flies up and up over the tree tops. When I'm big, I'm going to go to Africa to see the Goliath beetle.

GOLIATH BEETLE

Beetles are fun to watch. I wonder how many beetles are watching me.